GROW YOUR OWN

SWEET PEAS

Illustrated and designed by

Ley Honor Roberts

eden project

Getting started

Everybody loves sweet peas, with their pretty colours and gorgeous scent. People will think that you are very clever to grow your own. In fact, sweet peas are not hard to grow, and will do as well on a windowsill as in a garden. Here is what you will need to get started:

Seed compost

Available in bags from supermarkets and garages as well as garden centres. Peat-free is best.

Don't use potting compost - it's too rich for your seeds.

Gro-bags are a cheap way of buying seed compost.

Sticks

Bought from the garden centre (ask for pea sticks), or suitable ones that you pick up in the garden.

Seed pots

All these things make good plant pots for seeds.

Half a kitchen roll tube filled with damp soil works well for sweet peas.

Solid containers need drainage holes in the bottom. (Ask for adult help with this.)

Soak the seeds overnight for best results.

Water

Rainwater is best, but tap water will do.

Patience

The sweet peas will take about 12 weeks to get from seed to flower. Keep a diary to see how they grow each day.

Sowing your sweet pea seeds

The best time to sow

The best time to sow is between March and midsummer. After midsummer, the days get shorter and the plants don't have time to grow up and make flowers before the cooler days of autumn set in. You can also plant them in September and keep them over winter in a light, sheltered spot.

planting time   midsummer   flowering time

| Jan | Feb | Mar | Apr | May | Jun | Jul | Aug | Sep | Oct | Nov | Dec |

What to do

1. Fill your containers with soil. Don't worry about getting your hands dirty!

I'm planting my seeds in fibre pots in a seed tray.

2. Water the soil. Make sure that it is moist but not too wet – like a squeezed-out sponge.

3. Plant one seed in each fibre pot or section of an egg box, or one in each half of the cardboard tube. In a big container plant the seeds about 5cms apart.

Plant your seeds at twice their own depth.

Sweet pea seeds don't need light at first but the temperature needs to be above 6°c.

4. Cover the seeds with soil.

Like us, sweet peas need water, air and food to grow.
The sweet pea seeds get their water from the soil and food from inside their seed coats (which is why they are quite big). As they push above the soil they need light too.

From seeds to seedlings

Sunlight

As soon as your seeds start to sprout, put them in a sunny place. Turn each container every day so the seedlings don't bend one way towards the sun.

Watering

Water the seedlings so the compost stays damp. That might not be every day.
If the container is dripping, your seedlings will drown because they can't breathe.
If the compost is too dry the seedlings will die of thirst.
If they are nice and green and look good, you've got the right balance.

Talk to your seedlings! Encourage them.

Slugs and snails

Look out for slugs and snails – they'll be hiding in damp and dark places, such as under the pots. Get rid of them.

Preparing the ground for planting

(See the next page if you are growing your sweetpeas in big containers.)

1. Find a sunny spot.

While your seedlings are growing is the time to do this.

2. Remove the stones and big weeds.

3. Fork the soil over. Be gentle with worms – unlike slugs and snails, they are gardeners' friends, helping to dig the soil as they make channels through it, and helping to feed it with their poo!

Planting out your seedlings

In the garden

Remove seedlings from their small pots or tray.
Be very careful when you pull them up so as to not snap the roots.
Gently remove from the container, trying to keep as much soil
around the roots as possible.

> I can put this seedling in the ground in its fibre pot because it rots, so do eggboxes and cardboard tubes. You might need to shred them a bit first.

Try 'puddling in'

Make a little hole and fill it with water. Let the water drain away before planting the seedling.

Plant the seedlings in the soil

Plant them at the same depth as they were in the compost.
Press them in with your fingers but be careful not to squash the stem –
this is the plant's drinking straw for sucking up water from the soil.

In large containers

You don't have to have a big garden to grow sweet peas. You can grow them in a large pot or bucket or even in a window box.

Fill your container with compost (don't forget the holes in the bottom) and plant your seedlings in the same way.

Watering

Water your plants if it doesn't rain. Make sure the water goes down into the soil. Remember that plants in pots dry out very fast.

Sticks

Put a stick beside each seedling now. Put something on the end of the stick to protect your eyes, such as a bottle top, plasticine, tennis ball or a rubber glove.

Caring for your Sweet pea plants

Climbing frames

Here are some ways of supporting them if you have more room outside.
Make climbing frames for your plants from pea sticks, or trellis.

A wigwam is a good shape for a frame, whether you are growing
your sweet peas in the soil or in a pot. Push your sticks into the
ground in a circle and tie them together at the top.

How sweet peas climb

Sweet peas have long tendrils
that wrap around anything they
can find to pull the plant upwards
towards the sun.

If you have lots of room in your garden
you could make a tent-shape
frame from bamboos or sticks
from the garden.

When your sweet peas have
grown you will have a beautiful
and fragrant den to hide in.

Slugs and snails

Slugs and snails can munch through your seedlings overnight and ruin all your hard work.
Depending on the sort of person you are, you can

DISCOURAGE THEM

by making barriers
from hair cuttings, sand
or broken-up eggshells.

TRAP THEM

under upside-down
grapefruit halves. They
will hide there.

KILL THEM

in a jar or saucer of
beer. They will fall
in and drown.

More pests

APHIDS suck sap and spread disease, Get rid of these
pests by watering the plants with a weak solution of eco washing-up
liquid. Water them with a weak solution of liquid seaweed (from
a garden centre) as a tonic to help them get better.
Ask an adult to help you with this.

Lovely scented sweet peas

What to do with the flowers

Keep cutting the flowers – this encourages the plant to grow more. Pick off any dead flowers.

Make a gift

Tie a nice bunch with ribbon as a gift for the donor of this book!

Grow again

SWEET PEAS
eden project 20 Fragrantissima seeds

Save some seeds for next year. Leave them on a sunny windowsill for a couple of weeks to dry out. Use this packet again and stick it up.

Perfume and pot pourri

Use petals and water to make scented flower water.

Hang some bunches up to dry and use the dried petals for scented pot pourri.

pretty pictures

Make a colour palette from the different coloured flowers you have grown.
Make a picture from them. You could press it by covering it
with paper and putting it inside a heavy book for a couple of weeks.

Did you Know?

Meet the family

The pea family is large and varied. It contains:

annuals (that live for one year) – like sweet peas,
perennials (that live for several years) – like lupins,
vegetables – like runner beans,
shrubs – like gorse,
trees – like highly poisonous laburnum.

lupins

runner beans

gorse

laburnum

Most of them are easy to spot, because they have pods, flowers shaped like sweet peas, and finely-divided leaves.

Making protein from fresh air

Protein plants

Sweet peas are poisonous, but there are plenty of plants in this family that we eat all the time, such as lentils, peas, beans and chick peas. They are called pulses and they are useful in non-meat diets because they contain protein.

Friendly bacteria

Plants in this family make their own protein with the help of some friendly bacteria that live in their roots and feed on the sugars made by the plant. The bacteria mix nitrogen from the air (that reaches them through holes in the soil) with the sugars to make protein.

That's good for us, because even though the air we breathe is 78% nitrogen, we can't convert it into protein ourselves. We have to depend on the bacteria for that.

The Eden Project brings plants and people together.
It is dedicated to developing a greater understanding
of our shared global garden, encouraging us to
respect plants and protect them.

Other GROW YOUR OWN titles:

GROW YOUR OWN SWEET PEAS
AN EDEN PROJECT BOOK 1 903 91938 X

Published in Great Britain in 2005 by Eden Project Books, an imprint of Transworld Publishers

1 3 5 7 9 10 8 6 4 2

Text copyright © The Eden Project, 2005 Illustrations copyright © Ley Honor Roberts, 2005

The right of Eden to be identified as the author of this work has been
asserted in accordance with the Copyright, Designs and Patents Act 1988.

Eden Project Books are published by Transworld Publishers, 61-63 Uxbridge Rd, London W5 5SA
A division of The Random House Group Ltd
In Australia by Random House Australia (Pty) Ltd 20 Alfred Street, Milsons Point, Sydney, NSW 2061, Australia
in New Zealand by Random House New Zealand Ltd 18 Poland Road, Glenfield, Auckland 10, New Zealand
and in South Africa by Random House (Pty) Ltd Endulini, 5A Jubilee Road, Parktown 2193, South Africa

THE RANDOM HOUSE GROUP Limited Reg. No. 954009

Printed and bound in Italy

A CIP catalogue record for this book is available from the British Library.

www.kidsatrandomhouse.co.uk   www.edenproject.com